The High School Experience

Abbey Rodgers

BookLeaf
Publishing

India | USA | UK

Presentation by *BookLeaf Publishing*

Web: www.bookleafpub.com

E-mail: info@bookleafpub.com

ISBN: 978-93-5744-968-7

First edition 2022

DEDICATION

To Bella, for always believing in me

To Viv, for always sticking by my side

To Mom, for supporting me always

And to Rachel and Camila, you're eternally missed, and forever loved

freshman

freshman year, freshwater streams
the kids on my block, addicted to their screens

free walks during lunch, sparking up
leaves crunch

do i really belong here?

invited to a party, but grounded for suspension
sneak out through my window, trouble always
my intention

this party is home, and yet i've never felt so
alone

music i haven't heard before
people i'd never know i could adore

is this the life i've been missing? are these girls
so attached to the faces they're kissing?

high school life isn't really like the movies,
it's drinking with friends, it's feeling the beauty

but what is to come once i leave this old city,
will i dance with the rain? will i know what i'm
feeling?

i'm too young to know, and too old to care
ninth grade flew away, like the wind in my hair

pot

underneath a bridge i've just been acquainted
and will soon become good friends with

a large glass piece sits between my knees

new friends, eventually foes, crowd my
inhalation
anxiety pulls at my veins

burning sensation in my lungs

i cannot breathe, i cannot think

what's happening in my mind?

vision blurred and teleportation doesn't feel
impossible anymore

how did i get here again?

we eat, we smoke, we walk aimlessly

is this what i have been longing for?

no house, no home, just crisp air and untied
shoelaces

cool

i'd forgotten nearly half the memories
from back when we were cool
a time when parties were our remedies
cigarettes for lunch, smoking behind the school

if your parents were loose, buy a bag (maybe
two)
if the opposite strikes-shit! what have i got for
you..
"be discreet, if mom sees then we're both
fucking screwed"
relax, swallow this, all your dreams will come
true

a stolen bracelet dangles low
and it feels like not so many months ago
that them, you, and i said our goodbyes
and took the long way home

now my hair is a mess, and i don't know the day
how old am i again? did i throw my adolescence
away?
the hangover hurts, but you know it won't stay

the liquor you down, watch the world fade to
grey

back when we "knew" addiction meant you were
cool
and only the losers ever followed the rules
i know that we thrived when defiant in schools
but the kid you thought poor of, underneath he's
a jewel

i've seen sisters turn to stone
lively faces now, just skin and bones
i just want to help, your pain is my own
"whatever" you frown, turn, walk away. alone

alleyway romantics, parking lot fights
i'll remember our classics we'd belt through the
night
back when all of us knew, that we were the shit
"no, wait! not yet, the game's just started, don't
quit"

rejection

i am the goddess of rejection
blind with hate, and bound to hurt
the goddess of rejection waits
for fate to turn to dirt

and while my subjects are toiling, catering
rounds pearlescent garden gates
i reign eternal, bloody, aching
i can't ever make mistakes

the god of love, he speaks for me
and tells them i am okay
and if you are to disagree
know inevitably i'll cry

erida, my love, she watches me weep
corrosion strikes my heart
when fallen, my soul, only yours to keep
till those of them rip us apart

you

sinkhole soul, full cheeks
without these, thrown into the world, i'm
incomplete
what goes on behind those eyes?
what lingers beneath soft hair?

forever growing closer-words, smiles, touch
and yet evermore pushing away
why can't i read you? the pages out of order
letters misplaced and backwards
outward appearance flaunts ego
but what lies under?

on edge- my fault- i don't crave pity
i just wish i could know if you still find me
pretty
history i cannot rewrite; change never finds the
past
please baby, know i love you and want this love
to last

your kindness, i ache- how can i possibly relate?
to imagine a world that crushed hard to create
heart and hands made of gold
forever wish i could hold

i hold our time preciously, every date
i want to show you the world, before it's too late

<h1 style="text-align:center">second</h1>

another call refusing to go through
your call has been forwarded-
it hurts to feel so second best

i had asked to see you, and you agreed
why don't i keep my heart under my sleeves
i know to you, i'm only second best

when cigarette ash breaks from the unlit tobacco
the car rides turn to the same dust we kicked
from under our shoes

do you think of me as second best?
i know you do. i can't handle change

my art is so lackluster now since i stopped
abusing substances,
my personality feigns internal dread

do i wish to be alone?
no, but i cannot stand your company

do you wish i was dead?
i do. i know you wish I was like the others.

god, i pray to feel less than i do now,

the overwhelmed emotional response drives
them away,
and when you drove me home i know
you wish you'd left me stranded

my shoes are covered in mud and blood
they don't belong to me.

i wish i wasn't second best

love

the worst part about falling in love is realizing
you're in it
that you are helpless, floating in a vast ocean
scrambling and reaching
for the boy you swore you would spend the rest
of your life with

he knows all the words to your favourite songs
the ones you can't even listen to anymore
they're a reminder of what could have been

your hands on his back in the basement of an
unknown house
it's so cold, but you warm up to the idea of your
eyes locked in his
if winter brought us together, will spring tear us
apart?

the worst part about falling in love is having to
do it all over again
at a station that felt like home base, you let him
get to second
you can see each other in the old married
couples as they walk to their cars

now he's driving his, the streetlights and stars
look so beautiful atop the cemetery
fireworks feel like two lips holding on, and
friends became family tonight
like always, seasons change, and your love
hibernates and hopes to breathe again

the worst part about falling in love is trying to
hold onto it
this is the one, your other half
a perfect puzzle piece, completing your every
day

so maybe he returns your calls and soon you
can't sleep without hearing his voice
he holds you as if he'll never let go, and when he
says he loves you, he means it
your aching sadness goes away, and you know
his does too

as seasons change, days become routine
he misses you more as you miss him less
are the days as colourful as before?

you fall into steps like dancers:

eat, smoke, sex, repeat

he doesn't feel comfortable anymore

when your goodbyes have been said, things
exchanged, love shrivels and dies
you cannot sleep, you cannot eat
you wonder if the problem has been you all
along

but you're wrong
your love isn't meant for just one person

the worst part about falling in love is the fear of
losing your capability of loving
love is not a whimsical dream existing only in
fiction
it is a shared experience we can encounter
whenever we deem fit

while love is not in your control, you can find it,
not only in certain circumstances
but in everything
you must let yourself love again

infatuation

this relationship worked when we were both
infatuated with each other
when the sky turned purple and the thought of
you instantly crossed my mind

i could see us both staring at the stars in my
backyard
if the sky changes now, that bittersweet ache
stings my tongue
tasting sick lemon and sour tobacco felt so good.

when i tried to teach you to play guitar,
your fingers beneath mine and intertwined,
interconnected between hands

look at where we came from-
fighting for the other's attention
holding it tightly
a child holds their comfort in the way i held you
late at night.

the way your lips felt on my skin and whispered
that i would be okay
promising my sadness and disparity to
disappear-
you were right for a little bit

bite at my skin and cradle me in your arms
fearful of what was to come next

but when we lost the spark

that ember held everything

as quickly as it appeared,

it was gone

questions

when will the world stop spinning so fast?
if it ever stops spinning at all
i'm growing up quicker than i ever imagined
will yesterday grow legs and run farther away?

last year is last month is last week
did i throw away my youth?
wishing, waiting, wondering for tomorrow

but eventually i'll run out of tomorrows
has the clock run out? Am i out of time?
it's 11:11, and my wish is to turn back
to run away from responsibility and indulge in
escapism

next week becomes next month becomes next
year
what happened to tomorrow?
longing, lusting, living for yesterday

party

the life of the party doesn't wait for happy hour
none of the twenty-four are, so why wait?
if the bottle is cracked
no strings attached
today has been the best day

so mommy's been worried about my abuse
and "school's just ended" is a worn out excuse
i promise my life isn't going down the drain
i need to play music, it drowns out the pain.

when midnight strikes in eight-plus hours
and the clouds have been screaming "please, just
shower"
the life of the party downs another upper
and walks downstairs to not eat any supper

nothing is lonelier than a party where you know
no one's name
but everyone knows yours, "riot", "druggie" a
claim to fame
they don't know who you are, and neither do i
just sit and make out with a brand new guy

he's tall and he's older
won't cry on your shoulder
and always makes sure you'll never be sober

if i drink anymore, i think I'll explode
the mind and... everything aches to implode
my makeup is smeared, and we're out of bacardi
this is what it's like to be the life of the party

home

this is the place i grew up
drank my first bottle, spilled my first cup
this is the house i called home as a kid
but now when i look at it- the things that i did

we used to get rowdy, in the basement i dwelled
the first time i cried, you were the one- i raised
hell
and i'm sure when i leave i'll feel much less
alone
but it's not like an old friend you can call on the
phone

if home is where the heart is, then mine must be
misplaced
all i can see in this empty shell
are the memories i wish i'd erased

the kitchen held birthdays for all of us kids
the christmases spent when my laughs hurt my
ribs
all of these things i don't want to let go
but to stay here for longer, just unattainable

when you met my mom, and she thought you
were sweet

and ten days later you left me crying in the street
and i know when i leave i won't feel so alone
but this house isn't someone i can call on the
phone

this place, all i've known my whole life
but maybe if i leave i'll feel more than alright
nightmarish memories plague through the vents
to leave right away, it only makes sense

frankly

if i can be frank for a moment: i don't see the
point in living like this.

the love i've received doesn't feel deserved
this aching hole in my chest
it's overwhelming
everything i have ever wanted has slipped
through my fingers

do i truly wish for happiness or do i wish for the
end?

consciousness is a burden we all bear
self-actualization says i am ineligible
dark holes puncture my brain
enveloping serotonin
morphing any happiness i feel into great and
unmatched despair.

so what, you say i'm talented?
but this is just a front
it is a toxin that executes blind faith
troubling me and my person

for when will you realize it has been a dream?

crafted by my subconscious and perpetuated by
my desire to be better
i lack the aspirations i once used fulfill my every
day
i used to dream to paint every wall
i used to pound on my desk
craving the sky to be a shameful colour of deep
indigo
of my own creation

i look for love in every corner of the world
and while i once found it in every hollow
alleyway or empty room
now it doesn't even cross my mind
shadows lurk in vacant paintings
in free parking spaces

they've no home
i've no home.

worthless wasting space
uninhabited beds that once held sleeping
children
i was that sleeping child
whisked away from under the covers into lands
of cherry trees and strawberry bushes.

when the room is lit by unscented candles
the world stops its continuity

the moon and stars reflect their light onto a
south-facing balcony
and the colour in your eyes shifts from green to
blue and back
everything but the earth spins into a loveless
circle
encapsulating what could have been
rejecting what will be

your lonely heart will never feel the same.

he's new and shiny
older just by a few months but also by years of
unshared experience and troubles
your hair is a different colour again

forgiveness is a newfound skill
hate only travels with you if you let it

if you disregard the joy you once felt you won't
ever feel it again

have you felt this happy in years?
or is it a facade created by new love, new
friends, new seasons?
you don't know and can't care

but inside, a part of you wishes it had all worked
out.

why are you so afraid of happiness?
why, when the sun sets and the sky opens up
do you ache to see someone old- with their
ugliness and impermanence?
why, after everything that has happened, do you
crave how you once felt

he made you so sad, but to be happy is
uncomfortable

do you fear light?
do you fear impending rain and showers?
all they ever seem to bring in summer is daisies
and dandelions
the weeds that grow on front lawns-
their toxicity you crave
their "wrong place, right time" semblance.

when he laughs, why do you wish to stop
loving?
are you afraid to laugh along?
if you do, does the idea frighten you into a state
of nocturnal disaster?
the night is calm and forgiving
the day is cruel and unjust

but what is your justification for unhappiness?
are you afraid of absolution?

are you as evil or tough-skinned as those around
you believe?

he is gone now, and so am i
blown away with the wind and into electrical
lines
stinging my limbs and asking,
"how did you get here? do you still believe in
love?"

i don't

isolate

the indescribable intoxicated emotion
isolation

starting in the palms, electrifying through the
fingertips
building strength in the empty replies

reminding the self "you are here to please,
nothing requited"
they care for those who make sense

and eat the hearts of the misunderstood

reiterating the tales i've been told since time
began
but i see beneath their pity

destiny doomed me, a person to hold up the
greatness of others
and fall back into the hollow abyss some call
hope

hopeful today is the day i'm noticed

hopeful the exceptional isolation turns into
inclusion

hopeful of myself

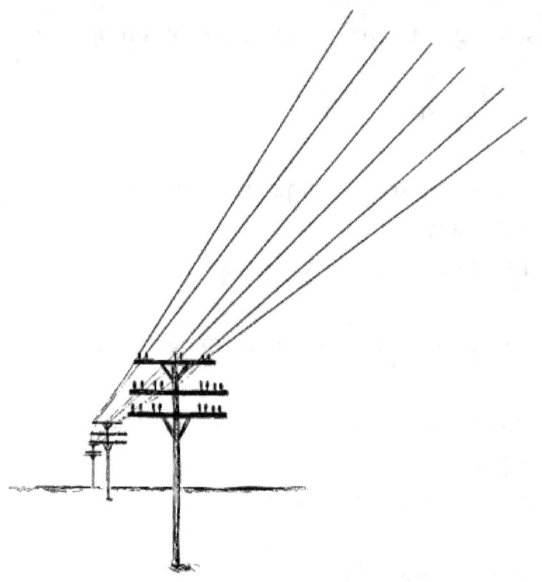

smile

it's dark in my room though the lights are turned
on
storm clouds overhead, i play your favourite
song

it's been six-ish months since you passed away
but everyday morphs together the same

i think about you first thing in the morning
i forget all about the past, i forget that i'm
mourning

your bright soul shines behind my eyes
i wished i could have said goodbye

if i lose focus on the task at hand
i feel thousands of bricks on my back
understand?

if i told you that night that i loved you the most
if i knew one petty fight would lead to overdose

would you tell me you loved me, even if it's a lie
i don't feel anything, anymore inside

if i close my eyes i can still see your smile

almost a year you've been gone, my it has been a while

since we talked, but i know that it feels like yesterday
but it's not and i worry i will forget your face

sleep

sleeping seems to be the only thing i'm good at
nowadays
cold air blowing in from the west chills my
bones
blankets can only soothe so much

i'm begging to be underground, praying to a god
i know doesn't exist
maybe he'll listen today or tomorrow, but
yesterday was too much to ask

anniversaries wish to be remembered, but i'd kill
to forget for just one silly little day,
for one silly little day.

mother thinks i'm too beautiful to be this sad,
she doesn't understand that beauty is irrelevant
when the days get shorter and nights become all
i need

my breathing becomes unbearable,
the air becomes thick and wet
i miss when we used to disintegrate together

am i condescending? am i getting insufferable
again?

do i push away everything i've ever loved and
leave just my shadow?
she sees how intolerable i'm becoming and still
refuses to leave.

why? i ask. why don't you understand i'll only
heal once i've been alone for so long, that
nothing fazes me anymore?

should i just go back to sleep?

38

birthday

one year ago today, september 9th, you asked
my name
i replied kindly, we exchanged our plans for the
day
"would you like to come over, i've got weed and
drink lets get un-sober,"
and with you is how i spent the entirety of
october

i used the city transit bus, it sent me to your old
address
i thought i might start crying on the spot

sometimes i sit and wonder if i really could have
helped
it was your birthday but i watched you fade
away, like someone else
breathe in slow, i swear i'll choke if i think any
longer
i know you're strong, i wish i could be stronger

7 ugly fucking months have past, i barely hear
your name
i've wondered what life would be like if it all
just stayed the same

painful memories reminded, I suppose i'm still insane
but maybe just one of these days i'll wake up
with no pain

drawings that you kept from me, placed nicely in
your folder
you left pieces of my heart in there, now i'm
growing colder
and in the meantime i will learn that nothing
lasts forever
and hopefully march 10th next year will bring
just sunny weather

food

im just so fucking hungry
but it's filling a hole with individual grains of
rice
i don't want to feel full, i don't want to feel food

i don't want to feel, period

i bet she doesn't cringe at the sight of her
lunches
or she can ask all her friends to go out to
brunches
and hey, maybe i'd like to do girly things too
but they radiate yellow, and i'm a cautious blue

forgive me my darling, i didn't mean to
disappear
it's just... things are happening... voices scream
in my ears
i'm so tired of living and living is my curse
don't tell me how much my life to some kid
would be worth

your hardest isn't good enough, wow, why what a waste
of organs, breath, brain, and bones, merely excess space
don't look at me like that, like i'm someone you hate
i know you don't love me, your distaste is my fate

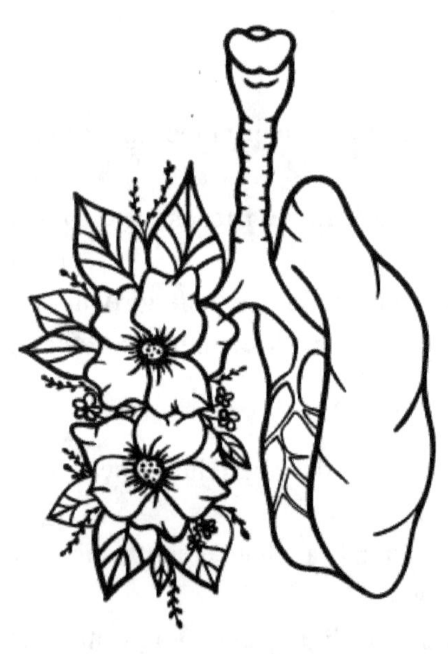

coping

i've quit what i once used to cope
though the thoughts ricochet restlessly
it's easy now
to ignore the whispers
to disregard my old thinking patterns

but it wasn't before

i was high out of my mind
all of the time
putting scars on my body
relapse after reasons

a decaying form, i used to hold
body frail, skin frozen cold

the saddest music could have saved my soul
the only thing that helped
i wish to hold the old me

history can repeat itself
of this, i am aware

but for now, i'll enjoy the weight lifting off my
chest
i'll clutch the hope i've created for myself

i hope to heal
i will get better

lessons

the universe puts people together for a reason
each person in your life is meant to teach a
lesson
that lesson could be love
or hate
or remorse
or indifference

the universe brings someone into your life
present for 3 years
in and out, in and out, in and out
you still love them regardless of status
you still remember, with songs that you both
loved
you still remember, even though they don't

the universe brings someone into your life
possibly the same individual who broke you
and the burning, bubbling, boiling rage
you hate them for their part in your pain
you hate them for your part in their pain

the universe brings someone into your life
and now you don't rely on them for happiness
affection, lost, affection, lost again
you're sorry for ever believing you did

you're sorry for the inconvenience of loving you
you're sorry for their feelings

the universe brings someone into your life
for the first time in what could be forever
look at me, look at me, look at me
their apathy for your well being
their apathy for your overwhelming feelings
your apathy of life without them

the universe brings these people into your life
each person teaching a lesson
teaching you to love
to hate
to forgive
and to forget

beauty

beauty is in every cracked sidewalk
every meter where ants scavenge
their discoveries back to the hill
they are determined to overcome obstacles and
every one is cherished
they all have a role to play.

in the weeds that grow between cement tiles
though a fortified man stands in their way
they persevere and thrive, even in their found
homes
they spring dandelions or crabgrass
abundantly in backyards
creating and sharing a story of persistence
encouraging us to do the same

in the street lights at night
the view of the ferris wheel with fireworks
exploding behind
i find beauty in her face
 her hands when we're sitting next to each other
a bench holding our exhausted bodies
we speak about who's sleeping with who
about how chilled our bones are
it's a beautiful feeling to not care about either

you are with exactly who you want to be with
right now
therefore the place doesn't even matter.

even in an empty room
beauty exists in the memories created there
it plays back the pictures on walls and hides
under the covers
waiting for the moments to come again... if they
ever will

i try to see beauty in all little things
every arbitrary knick-knack
the butterflies overhead
the moment between two lovers who have just
met
having no idea of the time they'll share.

wind blowing through an autumn night.

if you look for love in every place one can exist,
you'll find it

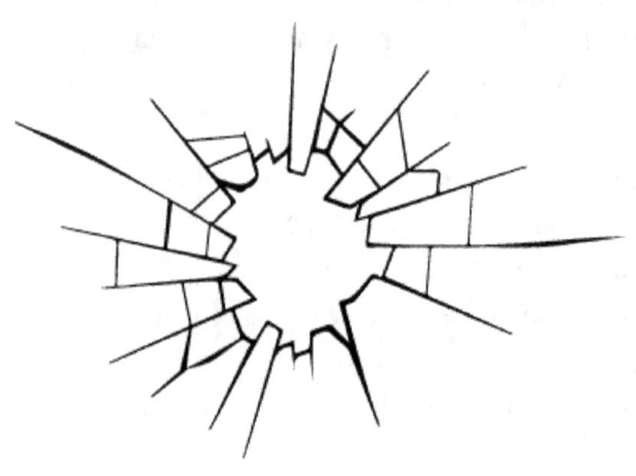

advice

little girl with yellow hair
don't let your dreams be feared
spend every moment awake, aware
and of life, don't dare steer clear

little girl with big blue eyes
don't let them take advantage
your intellect is not surprised
your heart and mind will manage

little girl who's growing up
don't take things way too far
his words build up, my buttercup
start coin collections in jars

little girl you're older now
i can't quite call you young
a perfect life, i'd disallow
smoke befriending your pierced tongue

little girl, i love you still
though friends or family leave
don't ever stop, so strong in will
you'll make it i believe